FROM MY HEART TO YOUR HEART

A Collection of Personalised Poems

Written by
Carrol Ramona Patterson

From My Heart To Your Heart:

A Collection of Personalised Poems

Copyright © 2025 by Carrol Ramona Patterson
Published in the United Kingdom by
Listening To Your Voice Publishing
The moral right of the author has been asserted.

All rights reserved. No part of this book may be reproduced, stored in a retrieval system, or transmitted in any form or by any means, electronic, mechanical, photocopying, recording, public performances or otherwise, without the written permission of Carrol Ramona Patterson Estate except for brief quotations embodied in critical articles or reviews.

Front cover image by Pexels

The right of Carrol Ramona Patterson to be identified as the author of this work has been asserted in accordance with sections 77 and 78 of the Copyright Designs and Patents Act 1988.

Because of the dynamic nature of the Internet, any web addresses or links contained in this book may have changed since publication and may no longer be valid. The views expressed in this work are solely those of the author and do not necessarily reflect the views of the publisher, and the publisher hereby disclaims any responsibility for them.

British Library Cataloguing in Publication Data: A catalogue record for this book is available from the British Library.

ISBN: 9781915327574

Book Cover Design: Listening To Your Voice Publishing

Editor: Annette Ruth Pearson

Typesetter: Annette Ruth Pearson

Table of Contents

Acknowledgements 5
Introduction 6
Lydia 7
Carolina 8
Welcome 10
The Power of Jesus' Love 13
At The Foot of The Cross 15
A Time to Act 16
What Kind of Friend Are You? 19
What Is Community Services? 22
Tears Come To My Eyes When I See The Homeless On The Streets 24
Thank You, God 28
Mother's Day 31
Family 33
The Trinity 36
The Holy Trinity Through Nature 38
The Beauty Of Springtime 40
The Sabbath 42
About The Author 45

Acknowledgements

The late Carrol Patterson, the wife of Kingsley Patterson, wrote the book you are reading.

Kingsley would like to express his deep appreciation and gratitude to Carrol for her creativity and inspiration, as well as the legacy she has left in these poems.

He would like to thank Oneta Letang for her help in compiling the poems and assisting in putting this book together, with the support of Annette Pearson, the publisher from Listening To Your Voice Publishing.

Finally, I would like to express my gratitude and praise to God for all that He has done in our lives.

Introduction

The idea for writing this book started when Carrol Patterson began writing her inspiring poems.

Initially, Carrol wanted to get her work published in a book, but at the time, she did not know how to do so.

Sadly, Carrol passed away in 2022 before seeing her dream realised.

Now, in honour of her memory, her Husband, Kingsley Patterson, has endeavoured to make her dream a reality.

Kingsley hopes you will enjoy reading her collection of personalised poems entitled *"From My Heart To Your Heart."*

Lydia

———— 99 ————

*L*OVELY and talented you are. The LORD LOVES and takes care of his own. You His child are not alone. He is always with you everywhere and at Home.

*Y*oung, beautiful, and petite. A perfect Beauty. and so very Sweet. Your Saviour, you wait patiently to see, to meet, and to greet. There will be Joy, No hiding, Nor Retreat.

*D*O ALL, you can, that is good in this life. As you wait in anticipation For a more spiritual and better Eternal Life with Christ.

*I*N ALL things aim to please GOD. AND take heed of the HOLY SPIRIT, Pleading, Teaching, and instructing. That will make your Life more enjoyable and interesting.

*A*LWAYS, ANGELS surround and protect you, and little Joan, Your Husband, so far away. GOD will take you both to him, and little one on the way, Where you all will be together happy and blest, in every way and in GODS CARE.

Carolina

— 99 —

*S*ING as you journey along. Your New Year, Has just began. BIRTHDAY Greetings, have just started. Sit back and enjoy this your special day. May God's rich blessings be with you all the way.

I GORGEOUS, Do you have a little time to spare, I wrote this poem for you my DEAR. because I care, It is a special gift sent to you, from me, as you can see.

*S*ALVATION is yours, The Saviour say, (Your reply) LORD help me to be willing to listen, and to obey. And to always Pray, that the HOLY SPIRIT WILL GUIDE ME TO You each and every day.

*C*HRIST is your strength, And your strong tower. He keeps you safe, from all harm and horror, He gives you overcoming power. For he is your strong tower, and deliverer.

*O*N CHRIST THE SOLID ROCK YOU MUST CLING, He gave you that stamina, to survive and sing. That inner strength, that zing, that will make you stand out in that special ring.

READY And willing, Reliable, and kind. Never a frown. ALWAYS beaming with an affectionate smile. That's your special gift. Your Love, and Kindness, you share with your loved ones, and all mankind. You are sublime.

LOOKING at life, GOD have made you strong, even though at times, things have gone wrong. But GOD gives you the strength to carry on. Making you stalwart and strong.

IN Your time spent with the LORD, He has richly blessed you. With sound mind, and talents that are sublime. GOD, Your heavenly father, gave you the wisdom to prosper and climb.

NOW listen my dear sis, (can't you hear?) Your protecting guardian Angels, are singing a BIRTHDAY Cheer, as they celebrate with you, your Birth, NEW YEAR. A year older. Your blessed growth, In this space and Atmosphere.

ANGELS adore you, And are always close beside you, to guide and protect you. So always be strong. Be cheerful and live long. GOD keeps you safe. And never will he fail you. HIS love is forever.

HAPPY BIRTHDAY! SIS, CORLINA!

Much love, XXXXXXX Stay Blest. Bro, Kingsley & Sis, Carrol,

Welcome

— 99 —

WELCOME, welcome to Dagenham Sabbath School. There, we come together to study and to learn God's Holy Rule and to enjoy our midday service, which will be soon.

And please do not forget A.Y.S. this afternoon. I am sure, as the youngsters would say, it will be cool.

ENJOYABLE and refreshing, you will agree. As you watch and listen to the children's performance, you will see how much effort they put into their programme for you and me. With open minds, we listen and learn about God's goodness, love, His will for us, and what He wants us to do. And how to give our gift, time, and talents to.

LEARNING their lines took much practice, patience, and time. So please say a hearty Amen at the end of their lines. Love is a gift sent from God above. The youth will demonstrate love today.

CHRISTIAN brethren, we should all be loving, and kind, and in perfect harmony and as of one mind. Christ Jesus is our example, a friend to us all. It doesn't matter who or what we are, large or small, short or tall, and how sinful we think we are.

ON Christ the solid rock we stand, for he is always there with his outstretched hands, waiting to pull you to his bosom, where you belong. Listen to the Holy Spirit pleading. As he bids you take the stand, holding unto the Saviour's Hand. Accept him today, my friend, that would be grand.

MOMENT by moment, you will see how much God is blessing you and me. He gave his son Jesus Christ, who bled and died on Calvary, to save poor sinners like you and me, so on bended knees we should always be, praising and thanking God for life, and his mercy.

ETERNITY awaits us. What will it be? Singing the triumphant song with Jesus and the Angels in harmony, or crying in pain and agony. That would be a terrible irony. Jesus is pleading Come to Him now. Please do not delay, my friend, for tomorrow might not come. Visiting friends and members, too. We hope you will enjoy worshipping with us here in Dagenham on this Holy and blessed Sabbath day. So, sit back and enjoy the programme planned for you! And remember we love you and God's blessing Be forever with you.

Visitors are welcomed guests who brighten up the place and bring with them much joy and good cheer.

Friends are like antique furniture. They are special and real; you never want to part with them.

Members are a special part that makes up a family unit. And without one of you, the unit wouldn't be the same.

Willing and able, we gather here to serve God IN love and not despair.

Everywhere we look, we see smiles and good cheer, for Jesus is here.

Love is of God, who is merciful to us and shows us He cares.

Church is his dwelling place, where we come to meet him face to face.

On bended knees we ask for mercy, and for his dwelling grace.

Members and Friends, Welcome, and may God bless you in every way, in

Everything you say and do, may it be to his love, honour and glory.

Brethren, greet your visitors, make friends, say hello to the one beside or next to you, and greet each other with a smile.

May GOD's richest blessings be poured out upon you. Happy Sabbath to you & yours!

The Power of Jesus' Love

Jesus is our Saviour and our sin bearer too.
He has set an example for us to follow, and to do.
The bread He broke, The cup He took,
(Holy Communion, Set out for us, in the open good book.)
It reminds us of His broken body, His shed blood.
His example He left us that we might do good.

Humanity He has taught us, by washing His disciples' feet. That we too might do the same, and wash one another's feet. That we might learn to show true humility, at home, and on the street. So brethren, let's learn from this day forward, what true humility, and Holy Communion is all about. Our Saviour paid that great price, for mankind.
"We the down and outs!"

Jesus our redeemer, paid the price, as a Sinner, His shed blood, on Calvary's Cross, that we might be a winner. Hope He gave us, amidst eternal loss. His love He unloaded, His grace He bestows, His love for us grows, and grows. His grace He has given to the human race. That you and I might have a better place. With love, and great pride, He bled and died, to save you and I, from shame and disgrace.

The love of Jesus shines bright. He gives us much joy and delight.

The birds and the bees, the flowers, and the trees, They are all precious in His sight.

The birds and the bees, they know His tender love and care,

The flowers, and the trees, they grow in splendor, that shows His love.

The insects, the animals, and the reptiles too, flourish on Jesus' love, like you and I do.

Jesus loves everything we see, that moves on land, and sea.

Like the fish, the animals, and you and me.

He is Our light, He shines bright,

He shows His love, in the moon, and stars at night, That shines above so bright.

Jesus has given us a new lease of life, and have made us free!

He takes care of us all, wouldn't you agree?

Remember always that Jesus our Saviour, Redeemer, and soon coming King, Has paid the great price, His self-sacrifice.

And have made us conquerors with Him, in this life, and the life to come.

Eternal life with Him in Paradise – Our Lord and Saviour Jesus Christ.

Composed by: C. R.

At The Foot of The Cross

———— 99 ————

At the foot of the cross, you must always stay, right beside Jesus your Saviour, who has shown you the right way. Give him your all night and day. As you depend on him to show you the right way.

The Holy Spirit will help you along your Christian pathway to be successful and achieve your goals in whatever way.

So hold on to the Saviour, Dear name. I pray. I am very proud of you; you have made the right choice today. Darling, I love you, hold fast, and stay true.

A Time to Act

— 99 —

A time to act, "Why is that"?

Jesus is coming soon, get ready before His impending doom. Now is the time to act, please don't forget that, His coming is a known fact.

A time to act, "Why is that"?

Life is short without a doubt. There is no guarantee that we will all be about.

A time to act, "Why is that"?

See the Bible for all the known and unknown facts. Please read it, study it, and make sure you don't relax.

A time to act, "Why is that"?

The children will demonstrate just that. Why? or why not?

Good morning, visiting friends, and members too. Today is a day for togetherness, laughter, and much praise.

So with songs and thanksgiving, let us worship the Most Holy One.

We are here today to celebrate with the children on their

children's day.

The children have a special programme planned for you.

The topic for the day is a time to act.

Friends, we know that Jesus is coming soon, and that is a fact.

Let us make ourselves ready for when he comes back.

Welcome, welcome, to Dagenham Sabbath School.

Where we come together to study and to learn God's holy rules.

And to enjoy our mid-day service, which will be soon.

And please don't forget A.Y.S. this afternoon.

I am sure, as the children would say, it will be cool.

Enjoyable and refreshing, you will agree,

as you watch and listen to the children's performance,

you will see how much effort they have put into their programme

for you and me.

Learning their lines took much practice, patience, and time.

So please say a haughty "AMEN"! At the end of their lines.

Love is a gift sent from God above,

The children will demonstrate today that love,

So, visiting friends, and members, too.

Sit back and enjoy the programme, planned for you!

What Kind of Friend Are You?

What kind of friend are you!?

What kind of friend are you?

Are you a faithful Christian friend?

Who will be there for me, from the beginning to the end?

Regardless of what I may do, to upset and displease you.

What about if I constantly annoy and offend you?

What kind of friend are you?

Are you a faithful Christian friend?

Will you be there for me, whatever time it may be?

Even though you know that I will not be there when you need me.

What about when I only get in touch, because my need for you to help me in such.

I need you to help me to mend.

Will you be there for me, to the very end?

What kind of friend are you!?

Will you still be my friend, when all the time you are the one, that is always giving?

Knowing that you will never get back anything,

Or will you say, 'This is it, my lesson I've learned?'

No more being nice to someone so disturbed?

What kind of friend are you?

Will you say, I have had enough.

I will show you that I too can be horrible and tough.

This is it, I won't try anymore, you are on your own.

I won't be good to you anymore, you are on your own.

I won't be around to watch, or listen to your moans, and groans?

What kind of friend are you?

Are you loving, patient, tolerant, forgiving, and kind.

OR are you unloving, impatient, intolerant, unforgiving, and unkind?

What kind of CHRISTIAN FRIEND ARE you?

A friend of Jesus our Saviour, who is love, and all divine. OR a friend of the evil one, who gives us grief, and makes us pine all the time?

Think on it, my Christian friend, whose friend would you rather be?

Think on it my friends, whoever you are.

What kind of friend are you?

What Is Community Services?

---- 99 ----

Caring and sharing is our motto.

Opening our doors and offering help to those in need of help and sympathy.

Members commitment to serve the community.

Meeting with people and sharing the word of God.

United in doing good.

Never say no to those in need.

Idle not when there is work to do.

Turn sadness into joy by telling of Jesus's love.

Young and old can take part in making someone feel loved and secure. Sharing what we have with the less fortunate, regardless of how small.

Evening and morning, whatever the time may be, there is always someone out there needing to be fed, clothed and sheltered.

Remedy and rendering aid is our game, God is love, and we too must show the same.

Victory must be gained over poverty, drunkenness, and stress.

Injustice and inability to copy must be overcome. We are the ones to help make it come true.

Calvary is where Christ died because of his love for mankind.

Eternal life is what he offers us. We can take it with both hands joyfully.

Saviour he is called, who will put all suffering, want and poverty to an end. 'When the time is come'.

THAT IS WHAT COMMUNITY SERVICES IS ALL ABOUT.

Tears Come To My Eyes When I See The Homeless On The Streets

――――― 99 ―――――

Tears come to my eyes when I see the homeless on the street.

Women with barely anything on, sleep on the concrete.

Men and Women huddle together in one big heap,

When it is time for them to go to sleep.

What can I do for them? My heart skips a beat, seeing all those people sleeping on the streets.

Lord, how can I help them? I would like to be discreet.

Tears come to my eyes when I see the homeless on the street.

People are sleeping without covers, no blankets, and no sheets.

Those who are lucky might have a bench in the park,

but must patiently wait until it's dark.

What can I do for them?

My heart skips a beat.

Seeing all those people with little or no food to eat.

Lord, how can I help them? I want to be discreet.

Tears come to my eyes when I see the homeless on the street.

Nowhere to call their own, come rain, come snow, whatever the weather, they have no where to go.

Nowhere to call their own. They are all alone.

All they might have for warmth and comfort, maybe some newspaper, and cardboard boxes, for their covers, their blankets, and their sheets.

Lord, how can I help them? I want to be discreet.

Tears come to my eyes when I see the homeless on the streets.

Why are they there?

Is it because no one cares or understands?

For some, things were once very prosperous and grand.

It was not their plan to become homeless, pitiful and sad.

Not long ago, some were like you and I, successful and very strong.

It wasn't their plan for things to go wrong.

Feeding the homeless is a pleasure for me,

but they need more than food, wouldn't you agree?

Lord, how can I help them?

I want to be discreet.

I am sure they would rather be like you and me.

Having a home they can call their own,

Maybe a house, or a flat, with two rooms up and one down, and living in their own hometown.

What are you and I, and society doing, to relieve these people of their poverty, suffering and need?

We are God's people He will help us to succeed.

Lord, how can I help them? I want to be discreet.

Tears come to my eyes when I see the homeless on the streets.

Lord, how can I help them, with their poverty, want and need?

Give me the way and means, dear Lord, that I may succeed.

I want to be a blessing, but discreet.

I know that they would appreciate positive help, and it would be a blessing and a treat.

Getting them off the streets.

Lord help me to do my part, but discreetly.

Tears come to my eyes when I see the homeless on the streets.

Read: Isaiah 41:10-13. When someone is making life

difficult for you, and you are experiencing much trial and tribulation, those verses will give you much comfort and peace of mind.

Thank You, God

--- ❞ ---

Thank you, God, for your tender loving care. Thank you, God, for my dear brethren. A smile here, and a smile there, A smile that is so sweet and sincere at gladness,

The heart and make one cheer.

Thank you, God, for taking the time to care.

A new year begins in 1995. Thank you, God, for life spared. It is January and the first month of the New Year.

New Resolutions and pledges made sincere,

Thank you, God, for teaching me how to pray.

Thank you, God, for the blessed Sabbath days,

And for your protecting care always.

Sorry, God, I forgot my promise to be kind and to care,

And for making it such a sad affair.

Thank you, God, for taking the time to show us how to be kind and to care.

It's February, ah! How time flies, it is the second month of 1995.

Thank you, God, for your dear Son, Jesus Christ.

Thank you, God, for His shed blood sacrifice.

Thank you, God, for All Our sins forgiven.

Sorry, God, for the way that I have been living.

Thank you, God, for your special care.

March is here, the third month of the New Year.

Thank you, God, for my Bible, so sweet, there is no better food that I would like to eat.

Thank you, God, for the guidance of the Holy Trinity, Father, Son, and Holy Spirit, one in three.

Sorry, God, for the way I have treated thee.

Thank you, God, for making me and molding me.

Thank you, God, for the rest of the year. April to November, so bright and clear.

Thank you, God, for health and strength, and sickness too.

Thank you, God, for peace at length.

Thank you, good neighbours and friends,

Thank you, God, for peace at length, with you.

Thank you, God, for people who care.

How much they make my heart glow.

Thank you, God, for peace and love.

December is here, the last month of the year.

Thank you, God, for the four seasons of the year.

Thank you, God, for my Church family so dear,
For the good and the bad times we have had this year,
And loved ones far and near.

Sorry, God, for the unkind way we have treated each other.
Unknowingly from day to day.
Thank you, God, for how we have lived and used it.
Thank you, God, for your Son Jesus Christ.
Thank you, God, for our spared lives,
Thank you, God, for the almost closing chapter,
The end of 1995.

Mother's Day

———————— 99 ————————

*M*OTHER'S are special, I do agree, Mother's love their children, my mother loves me.

*O*N bended knees, day after day, my Mother would pray for wisdom, to train us, her children, in the right way.

*T*RUSTING in God has made her free, true to her loved ones she will always be.

*H*APPINESS loyalty and love. God gifts, sent to you Mother from his courts above.

*E*VERYTHING my mother does for us, her children, she does it with devotion, delight, and much love.

*R*EARING us, your children gives you pleasure and pride and makes you happy and bright.

*D*OING things for you, Mother Dear gives us, your children, pleasure and delight.

*E*VEN now at this time of your life, you worry and fuss, when you done see us.

*A*LL around you, look and see, your husband, your children, who loves you, wouldn't you agree?

*R*IGHT beside you Joy will stand, to give you comfort, support, and a helping hand. While the rest of your children, will do what we can, whenever we can. Or when we feel that we must. So please, don't fuss.

HAPPY MOTHERS DAY!

And God Bless you! Mother Dear.

Lots of love June XXXXXXX

Family

In the beginning, God made a man and a woman. He gave him to be a mate and companion.

The first family on Earth was Adam and Eve, as well as Cain and Abel.

They were meant to love each other and to have a stable relationship.

That is how God ordained it to be; that was His great plan, but that was altered when sin in man began.

With God in control, families are spared the weight of a significant load.

With the family of God, there are blessings to be had.

It's very sad to say, but some families today still squabble and fight.

Fear and bitterness, with all their might.

They have malice and spite, envy and hate, and do things to each other that are hard to anticipate.

Some families are special, a rare bond.

The love of a lifetime is something they hold dear.

A bond that gets stronger and stronger, year after year. Their relationship with each other is rock solid and firm.

Nothing can penetrate, for they are stronger than strong, and go on through storm.

In good or bad times, they all pull together, upholding and helping one another to get it together.

When the chips are down, they will always be around; they will comfort and coax.

They will never let each other down.

The family of God will never be unstable, for Jesus our Saviour,

He is at the head of each table, and he is always able.

The Holy Spirit instructs and teaches how to live, love, and forgive.

So, take care,

Remember that protecting angels are always near; don't give them cause for despair.

Families remember this:

A family that prays together is a family that stays together.

Salvation awaits them, God's blessings to be had,

which is more precious than earth's finest gold.

With God in control the whole family will have peace in their soul.

And a love for each other that will never get cold.

The Trinity

---- 99 ----

Jesus is and was God, one with himself at Creation – John 1:1-10.

Verse 10 explains it fully.

Jesus knew that man would sin, so He made preparations for man's fall.

There had to be truly a number one. So Jesus, who was and is still God, made His plan.

He would separate Himself from Himself;

He made a part of Himself higher, the ruler, God the Father.

And the other half, He became the Son.

And the Spirit which dwells in Him became the third part of the Trinity:

The Holy Ghost.

Jesus did that because of His love for all humankind.

He planned salvation for man.

He planned to become flesh as a man and die on the cross of Calvary for our sins.

And while He was doing that-for us there had to be one in

complete control:

God the Father – Jehovah God.

Think of it! If Jesus did not do that, when he gave up his divinity to save us, what would have happened to us?

How would Jesus overcome?

Who would be there to be in control, and all control?

And to master the whole universe while he was in human form?

(Do you get the picture?)

This was planned for us from the foundation of the world.

That is what the Lord revealed to me through the Holy Spirit.

I hope this explanation will help others to understand fully how much Jesus loves us.

And how the Trinity came about.

Thank you, Jesus, for my enlightenment. – Carrol L. Park

The Holy Trinity Through Nature

——— 99 ———

SON of GOD = JESUS (Seed)

GOD is the Trinity: 3 connected parts (Father, Son, Holy Spirit) = GOD

A full illustration of the Holy Trinity through nature:

A Bean Seed – stored in the Kidney Bean A whole Kidney Bean

Outer Layer (Skin) = GOD

The Bean splits & sprouts up a new tree Inside the bean = 2 "Seed" halves One Half = JESUS (Son of God)

Other Half = HOLY SPIRIT

Sprouting process:

The 2 halves (seeds) are joined inside the shell/skin So the 3 parts are 1 bean

This is like the Trinity

When the bean is planted, the shell breaks & the seed inside grows The seed gives birth to a new plant

So just like the seed (Son) gives birth to the tree, the Son gives birth to the Kingdom of God

Spiritual interpretation:

Just like the bean sprouts, the Son of God (Jesus) sprouted to bring forth eternal life

The seed must die to bring life (John 12:24)

The Beauty Of Springtime

———————— 99 ————————

The beauty of spring is that everything starts to come alive;
it springs up and thrives!
The birds sing their sweet melody, telling us that Spring is here.

Flowers are springing up everywhere: old ones, new ones, and those that are most rare.

The insects are scurrying everywhere, and the ants are looking for food that is so dear.

Animals are being born, two in a pair, new life that reminds us that there is always new.

But the beauty of Spring is the trees, that seem to come alive, their foliage, their leaves seem to burst out from inside,

And once more the beauty of God's creation comes fully alive, that man and beast may continue to flourish and thrive.

The heavens are clear, the sky is blue, God did all this for me and you.

The rain He sends is a blessing, a feast for man, beasts, and plants too. (for me and you)

The heavens come alive with birds of prey, all kinds of species, to light up our day.

Birds, bees, insects, reptiles, mammals and more.
We are all God's wonderful creation and plan.

So Lord Jesus, I pray, thank you for springtime, and this special day.

Father, Son, and Holy Spirit, I pray – Amen.

The Sabbath

---- 99 ----

The Sabbath is the Holy DAY OF REST. The day when we are especially blessed.

The DAY when the Godhead, Father, Son, and Holy Spirit, along with the heavenly HOST of Angels, come together with us, and our Protecting Angels to celebrate this special day of rest.

The Sabbath is a day when all Executives are extremely blessed.

It is a day when GOD's special People come together in His Temple to give Him thanks and Praise for all that He has done in the six days.

To seek His Wisdom in the best way we can. And to let others unify with God & everyone.

The Sabbath was made for man and not man for the Sabbath (Mark 2:27)

We must be sure about that! That's part of GOD's Special Plan, one of his special gifts to man. A Time of Pleasure shared with God and man. Studying His words, and communing with Him in much prayer, and giving Him Special Thanks and Praise.

The Sabbath is a time to reflect upon all the things we have and haven't done.

The good and the bad.

The things that made us happy or sad.

Our attitude in words, in thoughts and in deeds.

The waste of things we really didn't need.

The Sabbath leads us away from the world and into GOD's protective hand.

So He can make us strong, where the righteous stand.

With Jesus by our Side, we will ride the tide.

We will be Overcomers, we will not slide.

The Sabbath is the day when we can focus our hearts and minds on the last six days,

How we give Him thanks and Praise, and how we use our time and talents too.

Saying sorry for when we have failed.

Lord, please forgive.

And in His mercy, He will forgive, and make us live.

The Sabbath Day should be kept Holy. So we must take care.

Watch what we say and do.

We must be careful with our actions and our attitudes, too.

A time to reflect upon all the things we should have done, and didn't do. The things that allowed or wouldn't make us regret, feel sorrowful or fret.

The Sabbath is man's privileged day,

A day to share GOD's love,

And reflect on the things above.

With the family of God,

Our relatives, friends, and neighbours, too.

The gospel message He gave to me and you.

Our time and talents, too.

We must share the good news,

With those we meet on our way from day to day.

So, enjoy the Sabbath rest,

The special day that God has set aside and blessed. A day that God has given to man as a special gift, His day of rest.

Remember, Jehovah and His heavenly hosts are our special guests.

So please do not miss out on His love, celebration, and caress.

Friends, remember, on the Sabbath we are especially blessed.

About The Author

Carrol Patterson was born in Jamaica, St Andrews on 10 June 1944. She was the eldest of nine children.

Carrol arrived in England in 1960 and worked as a machinist. She married Kingsley Patterson on 27 September 1970. They had six boys and one girl.

Carrol grew up in the Seventh-day Adventist Church and expressed her love of Jesus by creating inspiring and encouraging poems. She started writing in the late 1970s to the early 1980s.

Carrol was also one of the founding members of the Clacton-on-Sea Seventh-day Adventist Church.